GLASSES ARE LOST.
I PROMISE I'LL NEVER DO IT AGAIN. EVER.
TODAY'S MY BIRTHDAY.
I NEVER HEARD YOU SAY THAT.
MY TOOTH IS LOOSE!
YOU'RE THE NICEST TEACHER IN THE WHOLE WORLD!
E IT.
I DON'T WANT TO.
DO I HAVE TO?
"And you thought your classroom was crowded."
SHE PUSHED ME.
I FORGOT IT.
I'M TOO TIRED.
IS TODAY LIBRARY DAY?
JUST BECAUSE.
READ IT AGAIN. JUST ONCE MORE!
NE'S ETTER.
I'M BLEEDING!
Marc Brown 1991

This Book of Days Belongs to

n *How a Book is Made* by Aliki.

The Art of Teaching

A Trumpet Club
Book of Days
1992

Published by The Trumpet Club
666 Fifth Avenue, New York, New York 10103

ISBN 0-440-84823-7

Art direction by Ann Hofmann
Printed in the United States of America
November 1991

1 3 5 7 9 10 8 6 4 2
KPH

Welcome to *The Art of Teaching*, our first annual Trumpet Club teacher's engagement diary. One year ago we decided to produce a special book for our teachers, something personal just for you. We decided to create a beautiful book full of original art, commissioned from twelve of today's most popular children's book artists.

Artists as diverse as Leo Lionni, Barbara Cooney and Aliki were delighted to join The Trumpet Club in this special tribute.

In addition to the lovely art to define each month, *The Art of Teaching* gives you biographies of the contributing artists, along with their personal reflections on teachers and teaching, a place to keep notes, plus important holidays.

Teaching is an art, and we hope this date book will remind you every day that we at The Trumpet Club are thinking of you and appreciate your work.

HAVE A
WONDERFUL YEAR

LYLE

work by Bernard Waber.

Artwork by Leo Lionni.

DECEMBER – JANUARY

December

S	M	T	W	T	F	S
1	2	3	4	5	6	7
8	9	10	11	12	13	14
15	16	17	18	19	20	21
22	23	24	25	26	27	28
29	30	31				

January

S	M	T	W	T	F	S
			1	2	3	4
5	6	7	8	9	10	11
12	13	14	15	16	17	18
19	20	21	22	23	24	25
26	27	28	29	30	31	

February

S	M	T	W	T	F	S
						1
2	3	4	5	6	7	8
9	10	11	12	13	14	15
16	17	18	19	20	21	22
23	24	25	26	27	28	29

LEO LIONNI

"A picture book is the result of thousands of apparently small, insignificant decisions. Yet the direction of a single brushstroke, the shape of the smallest pebble, the space between two leaves, the curve of a mouse's tail— as well as the sound of a vowel or the length of a word—play a determining role in the totality of the work. The ever-present challenge is to keep a firm grip on all the details while maintaining the vitality of the original idea."

MONDAY **30**

TUESDAY **31**

New Year's Day

WEDNESDAY **1**

THURSDAY **2**

FRIDAY **3**

SATURDAY **4**

SUNDAY **5**

From *Tillie and the Wall* by Leo Lionni.

JANUARY

January

S	M	T	W	T	F	S
			1	2	3	4
5	6	7	8	9	10	11
12	13	14	15	16	17	18
19	20	21	22	23	24	25
26	27	28	29	30	31	

ABOUT LEO LIONNI

Leo Lionni was born on May 5, 1910 in Amsterdam, Holland, and came to the United States in 1939. He has received four Caldecott Honor awards, for *Frederick*, *Swimmy*, *Alexander and the Wind-up Mouse* and *Inch by Inch*.

Leo Lionni believes that a good children's book should appeal to all people who have not completely lost their original joy in and wonder at life. He and his wife divide their time between a New York apartment and a 17th-century Tuscan farmhouse in Italy. He plays flamenco guitar.

MONDAY **6**

TUESDAY **7**

WEDNESDAY **8**

THURSDAY **9**

FRIDAY **10**

SATURDAY **11**

SUNDAY **12**

peace on earth an

JANUARY

January

S	M	T	W	T	F	S
			1	2	3	4
5	6	7	8	9	10	11
12	13	14	15	16	17	18
19	20	21	22	23	24	25
26	27	28	29	30	31	

NOTES

_____

_____

_____

_____

_____

_____

_____

_____

_____

_____

MONDAY **13**

TUESDAY **14**

Martin Luther King, Jr.'s Birthday

WEDNESDAY **15**

THURSDAY **16**

FRIDAY **17**

SATURDAY **18**

SUNDAY **19**

goodwill toward all men

From *The Alphabet Tree* by Leo Lionni.

JANUARY

January

S	M	T	W	T	F	S
			1	2	3	4
5	6	7	8	9	10	11
12	13	14	15	16	17	18
19	20	21	22	23	24	25
26	27	28	29	30	31	

NOTES

Martin Luther King, Jr.'s Birthday Observed

MONDAY **20**

TUESDAY **21**

WEDNESDAY **22**

THURSDAY **23**

FRIDAY **24**

SATURDAY **25**

SUNDAY **26**

Artwork by Jerry Pinkney.

January

S	M	T	W	T	F	S
			1	2	3	4
5	6	7	8	9	10	11
12	13	14	15	16	17	18
19	20	21	22	23	24	25
26	27	28	29	30	31	

February

S	M	T	W	T	F	S
						1
2	3	4	5	6	7	8
9	10	11	12	13	14	15
16	17	18	19	20	21	22
23	24	25	26	27	28	29

March

S	M	T	W	T	F	S
1	2	3	4	5	6	7
8	9	10	11	12	13	14
15	16	17	18	19	20	21
22	23	24	25	26	27	28
29	30	31				

JERRY PINKNEY

"The reason I draw today came from a project in the first grade when my teacher displayed my very large fire engine drawing on the bulletin board for fire prevention week and saw, she said, that I had a talent."

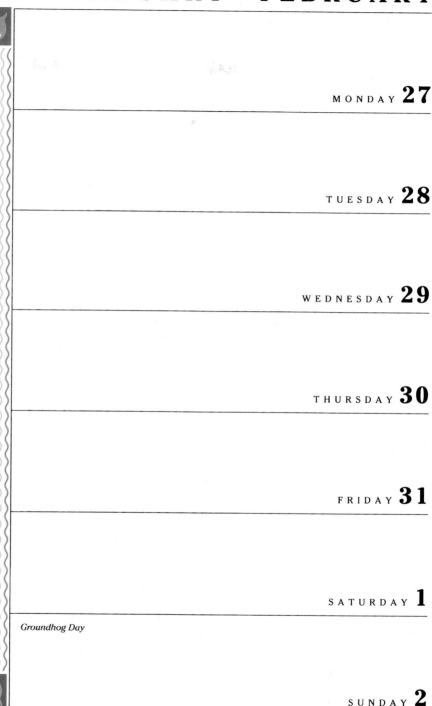

MONDAY **27**

TUESDAY **28**

WEDNESDAY **29**

THURSDAY **30**

FRIDAY **31**

SATURDAY **1**

Groundhog Day

SUNDAY **2**

From *Pretend You're a Cat* by Jean Marzollo,
illustrated by Jerry Pinkney.

FEBRUARY

February

S	M	T	W	T	F	S
						1
2	3	4	5	6	7	8
9	10	11	12	13	14	15
16	17	18	19	20	21	22
23	24	25	26	27	28	29

MONDAY **3**

Chinese New Year

TUESDAY **4**

WEDNESDAY **5**

ABOUT JERRY PINKNEY

Jerry Pinkney was born in Philadelphia, Pennsylvania, on December 22, 1939. He and his wife, Gloria, have four children, one daughter and three sons. His son Brian is also a children's book illustrator and his wife is a children's book writer.

Jerry Pinkney always researches his book projects intensively and uses photographs and live models for his illustrations. He has illustrated such picture books as *In For Winter, Out For Spring* and *Pretend You're a Cat* and won Caldecott Honor awards for *Mirandy and Brother Wind* and *The Talking Eggs*. A self-described slow starter, who loves music, he begins his day listening to classical music and works up to jazz in the afternoon.

THURSDAY **6**

FRIDAY **7**

SATURDAY **8**

SUNDAY **9**

From *Pretend You're a Cat* by Jean Marzollo,
illustrated by Jerry Pinkney.

FEBRUARY

February

S	M	T	W	T	F	S
						1
2	3	4	5	6	7	8
9	10	11	12	13	14	15
16	17	18	19	20	21	22
23	24	25	26	27	28	29

NOTES

_____

_____

_____

_____

_____

_____

_____

_____

_____

_____

MONDAY **10**

TUESDAY **11**

Lincoln's Birthday

WEDNESDAY **12**

THURSDAY **13**

Valentine's Day

FRIDAY **14**

SATURDAY **15**

SUNDAY **16**

From *Pretend You're a Cat* by Jean Marzollo,
illustrated by Jerry Pinkney.

FEBRUARY

February

S	M	T	W	T	F	S
						1
2	3	4	5	6	7	8
9	10	11	12	13	14	15
16	17	18	19	20	21	22
23	24	25	26	27	28	29

Presidents' Day

MONDAY **17**

TUESDAY **18**

WEDNESDAY **19**

THURSDAY **20**

NOTES

_____

_____

_____

_____

_____

_____

_____

_____

_____

_____

_____

FRIDAY **21**

Washington's Birthday

SATURDAY **22**

SUNDAY **23**

February

S	M	T	W	T	F	S
						1
2	3	4	5	6	7	8
9	10	11	12	13	14	15
16	17	18	19	20	21	22
23	24	25	26	27	28	29

March

S	M	T	W	T	F	S
1	2	3	4	5	6	7
8	9	10	11	12	13	14
15	16	17	18	19	20	21
22	23	24	25	26	27	28
29	30	31				

April

S	M	T	W	T	F	S
			1	2	3	4
5	6	7	8	9	10	11
12	13	14	15	16	17	18
19	20	21	22	23	24	25
26	27	28	29	30		

MARC BROWN

"When I was teaching, March always seemed the most trying of months. After a long New England winter, everyone in the classroom was suffering from cabin fever. March seemed the perfect month to plan something special to celebrate the arrival of spring—like a field trip! I always enjoyed the challenge of finding unique places that were not usually open to visiting classes. If you can live through March, you can endure almost anything!"

Bradley – conference 5:00

MONDAY 24

Beth – swim 5:00
piano 6:30

W.W.

TUESDAY 25

WEDNESDAY 26

Staff Develop. – p.m.

Gym.   Corwin Kron. – 7:00
ECFE

THURSDAY 27

Bethany – field trip – Mike pick
up 12:30

FRIDAY 28

Leap Year Day

SATURDAY 29

SUNDAY 1

From *Arthur's Teacher Trouble* by Marc Brown.

MARCH

March

S	M	T	W	T	F	S
1	2	3	4	5	6	7
8	9	10	11	12	13	14
15	16	17	18	19	20	21
22	23	24	25	26	27	28
29	30	31				

MONDAY **2**

TUESDAY **3**

Ash Wednesday

WEDNESDAY **4**

ABOUT MARC BROWN

Born November 25, 1946. Marc Brown is the creator of the Arthur adventure series, the latest of which is *Arthur Meets the President.*

Marc Brown has always loved to tell and listen to stories. He says, "Humor is an important creative element for me. I think children learn better when humor is involved in the teaching process." Marc Brown is married to Laurie Krasny Brown, who collaborated with him on *Dinosaurs Alive and Well*, among other books. In most of his books, the names of his three children, Tolon, Tucker and Eliza, are hidden in the art.

THURSDAY **5**

FRIDAY **6**

SATURDAY **7**

SUNDAY **8**

From *Arthur's Baby* by Marc Brown.

MARCH

March

S	M	T	W	T	F	S
1	2	3	4	5	6	7
8	9	10	11	12	13	14
15	16	17	18	19	20	21
22	23	24	25	26	27	28
29	30	31				

MONDAY **9**

Staff Develop. - a.m.
Dentist - 12:50

TUESDAY **10**

WEDNESDAY **11**

NOTES

_____

_____

_____

_____

THURSDAY **12**

_____

_____

_____

FRIDAY **13**

_____

_____

_____

SATURDAY **14**

_____

_____

SUNDAY **15**

From *Arthur's Tooth* by Marc Brown.

MARCH

March

S	M	T	W	T	F	S
1	2	3	4	5	6	7
8	9	10	11	12	13	14
15	16	17	18	19	20	21
22	23	24	25	26	27	28
29	30	31				

MONDAY **16**

St. Patrick's Day

TUESDAY **17**

WEDNESDAY **18**

NOTES

_____

_____

THURSDAY **19**

_____

_____

_____

_____

FRIDAY **20**

_____

_____

_____

_____

SATURDAY **21**

_____

_____

_____

SUNDAY **22**

From *Arthur's Baby* by Marc Brown.

MARCH

March

S	M	T	W	T	F	S
1	2	3	4	5	6	7
8	9	10	11	12	13	14
15	16	17	18	19	20	21
22	23	24	25	26	27	28
29	30	31				

MONDAY **23**

TUESDAY **24**

WEDNESDAY **25**

THURSDAY **26**

FRIDAY **27**

SATURDAY **28**

SUNDAY **29**

"Our neurotic cat, Athena, arrived one Halloween night at our barn looking very hungry. The only foods I could find that I thought a cat might like were light cream and chicken liver pâté. She liked them. She's been here ever since."

—MARC BROWN

Artwork by Barbara Cooney.

March

S	M	T	W	T	F	S
1	2	3	4	5	6	7
8	9	10	11	12	13	14
15	16	17	18	19	20	21
22	23	24	25	26	27	28
29	30	31				

April

S	M	T	W	T	F	S
			1	2	3	4
5	6	7	8	9	10	11
12	13	14	15	16	17	18
19	20	21	22	23	24	25
26	27	28	29	30		

May

S	M	T	W	T	F	S
					1	2
3	4	5	6	7	8	9
10	11	12	13	14	15	16
17	18	19	20	21	22	23
24	25	26	27	28	29	30
31						

BARBARA COONEY

Five Miracles:

"The Coming of Spring.

The Wonder of Things
Close By.

The Mystery of the Far
Horizon.

Clouds.

The Teaching of Even
One Person to Read."

MONDAY **30**

TUESDAY **31**

April Fool's Day

WEDNESDAY **1**

THURSDAY **2**

FRIDAY **3**

SATURDAY **4**

SUNDAY **5**

From *The Year of the Perfect Christmas Tree*
by Gloria Houston, illustrated by Barbara Cooney.

APRIL

April

S	M	T	W	T	F	S
			1	2	3	4
5	6	7	8	9	10	11
12	13	14	15	16	17	18
19	20	21	22	23	24	25
26	27	28	29	30		

MONDAY **6**

TUESDAY **7**

WEDNESDAY **8**

THURSDAY **9**

ABOUT BARBARA COONEY

Born August 6, 1917 in Brooklyn, New York. Barbara Cooney has illustrated over 100 books and has won two Caldecott Medals.

Barbara Cooney lives in Maine, is married to "an old-fashioned country doctor," now retired, and has four grown children. She says an artist needs the perfect tools, and since she's an avid gardener with the "most beautiful garden in town," she probably has just the right tools for gardening too.

FRIDAY **10**

SATURDAY **11**

Palm Sunday

SUNDAY **12**

From *Island Boy* by Barbara Cooney.

APRIL

April

S	M	T	W	T	F	S
			1	2	3	4
5	6	7	8	9	10	11
12	13	14	15	16	17	18
19	20	21	22	23	24	25
26	27	28	29	30		

NOTES

MONDAY **13**

TUESDAY **14**

WEDNESDAY **15**

THURSDAY **16**

Good Friday

FRIDAY **17**

First day of Passover

SATURDAY **18**

Easter

SUNDAY **19**

From *Miss Rumphius* by Barbara Cooney.

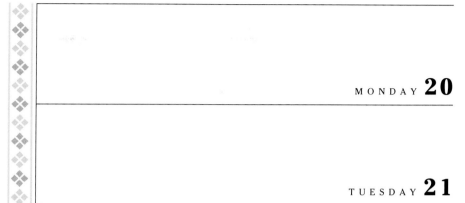

APRIL

April

S	M	T	W	T	F	S
			1	2	3	4
5	6	7	8	9	10	11
12	13	14	15	16	17	18
19	20	21	22	23	24	25
26	27	28	29	30		

NOTES

_____
_____
_____
_____
_____
_____
_____
_____
_____
_____
_____
_____

MONDAY **20**

TUESDAY **21**

Earth Day

WEDNESDAY **22**

THURSDAY **23**

FRIDAY **24**

SATURDAY **25**

SUNDAY **26**

Artwork by Al

April

S	M	T	W	T	F	S
			1	2	3	4
5	6	7	8	9	10	11
12	13	14	15	16	17	18
19	20	21	22	23	24	25
26	27	28	29	30		

May

S	M	T	W	T	F	S
					1	2
3	4	5	6	7	8	9
10	11	12	13	14	15	16
17	18	19	20	21	22	23
24	25	26	27	28	29	30
31						

June

S	M	T	W	T	F	S
	1	2	3	4	5	6
7	8	9	10	11	12	13
14	15	16	17	18	19	20
21	22	23	24	25	26	27
28	29	30				

ALIKI

"By kindergarten, I knew I needed to draw. By third grade, I knew I needed a dictionary.

"I've always loved words, but I've never been good at spelling them. Thank goodness my early teachers taught me the importance of the dictionary, and of looking up words. Not only did I find other unknown and fascinating words there, but it was my earliest form of research. I've had a dictionary on my desk ever since."

MONDAY **27**

TUESDAY **28**

WEDNESDAY **29**

THURSDAY **30**

FRIDAY **1**

SATURDAY **2**

SUNDAY **3**

From *How a Book Is Made* by Aliki.

MAY

May

S	M	T	W	T	F	S
					1	2
3	4	5	6	7	8	9
10	11	12	13	14	15	16
17	18	19	20	21	22	23
24	25	26	27	28	29	30
31						

ABOUT ALIKI

Aliki was born on September 3—she forgets the year—during the family's vacation in Wildwood Crest, New Jersey, although they lived in Philadelphia, Pennsylvania. She has written and illustrated over 40 books and illustrated many more, including books by her husband, Franz Brandenberg.

Aliki writes two kinds of books. Fiction—"feeling books which come from within," and nonfiction—"research books that come from the outside in, about subjects I wish to learn more about."

Aliki and Franz live in London and they have two children, Jason and Alexa.

MONDAY **4**

TUESDAY **5**

WEDNESDAY **6**

THURSDAY **7**

FRIDAY **8**

SATURDAY **9**

Mother's Day

SUNDAY **10**

In Elementary School we were marked for PERSEVERANCE. I learned the meaning of the word, and how to spell it, too.

(We were also marked for promptness, patience, cleanliness, kindness, cooperation, honesty ....)

Something I learned visiting schools.

Put another way:

TELL ME, I FORGET.
SHOW ME, I REMEMBER.
INVOLVE ME, I UNDERSTAND.

Ancient Chinese Proverb

I found that one in Newark, NJ airport!

We remember 10% of what we read, and 80% of what we do.

Have it. My Mommy taught me manners.

Thank you.

A Letter is like a kiss. You can read it again and again and again.

9×9=...

REMEMBER:

One may forget facts and equations, but one never forgets encouragement and love.

... 81

Great. You did much better.

Up, sluggard, and waste not life.

Ben Franklin said it.

In the grave there will be sleeping enough.

And someone else said:

"You teach by example."
"There's no such thing as 'can't'."
"Life is what you make it."

Artwork by A...

MAY

May

S	M	T	W	T	F	S
					1	2
3	4	5	6	7	8	9
10	11	12	13	14	15	16
17	18	19	20	21	22	23
24	25	26	27	28	29	30
31						

Nefertiti taught us how to live with a cat.

NOTES

_____

_____

_____

_____

_____

_____

_____

_____

_____

_____

"My kindergarten teacher told my parents I'd be an artist someday." —ALIKI

MONDAY **11**

TUESDAY **12**

WEDNESDAY **13**

THURSDAY **14**

FRIDAY **15**

SATURDAY **16**

SUNDAY **17**

From *We Are Best Friends* by Aliki.

MAY

May

S	M	T	W	T	F	S
					1	2
3	4	5	6	7	8	9
10	11	12	13	14	15	16
17	18	19	20	21	22	23
24	25	26	27	28	29	30
31						

MONDAY **18**

TUESDAY **19**

WEDNESDAY **20**

NOTES

THURSDAY **21**

_____

_____

_____

_____

_____

FRIDAY **22**

_____

_____

_____

_____

SATURDAY **23**

_____

_____

_____

SUNDAY **24**

From *We Are Best Friends* by Aliki.

MAY

May

S	M	T	W	T	F	S
					1	2
3	4	5	6	7	8	9
10	11	12	13	14	15	16
17	18	19	20	21	22	23
24	'25	26	27	28	29	30
31						

Memorial Day Observed

MONDAY **25**

TUESDAY **26**

WEDNESDAY **27**

THURSDAY **28**

NOTES

_____

_____

_____

_____

_____

_____

_____

_____

_____

_____

FRIDAY **29**

Traditional Memorial Day

SATURDAY **30**

SUNDAY **31**

JUNE

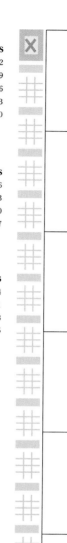

ROSEMARY WELLS

"I always loved the month of June best because behind me was school and indoor life, and before me was the summer spread out, full of salt water and sweet corn, big ripe tomatoes and my legs covered with scratches, bites and mud!"

MONDAY **1**

TUESDAY **2**

WEDNESDAY **3**

THURSDAY **4**

FRIDAY **5**

SATURDAY **6**

SUNDAY **7**

From *Hazel's Amazing Mother* by Rosemary Wells.

JUNE

June

S	M	T	W	T	F	S
		1	2	3	4	5	6
7	8	9	10	11	12	13
14	15	16	17	18	19	20
21	22	23	24	25	26	27
28	29	30				

ABOUT ROSEMARY WELLS

Rosemary Wells was born in New York City on January 29, 1943. She is the author and illustrator of over 40 books, including her well-known stories about Max and his bossy sister, Ruby.

Rosemary Wells is married and has two daughters, Victoria and Meg. She believes that a good teacher "is strict but has a vivid imagination and forgives our faults." As for her own work, she says, "Writing a story is like shining an old coin. The joy is in the polishing."

MONDAY **8**

TUESDAY **9**

WEDNESDAY **10**

THURSDAY **11**

FRIDAY **12**

SATURDAY **13**

SUNDAY **14**

From *Shy Charles* by Rosemary Wells.

JUNE

June

S	M	T	W	T	F	S
	1	2	3	4	5	6
7	8	9	10	11	12	13
14	15	16	17	18	19	20
21	22	23	24	25	26	27
28	29	30				

NOTES

MONDAY **15**

TUESDAY **16**

WEDNESDAY **17**

THURSDAY **18**

FRIDAY **19**

SATURDAY **20**

Father's Day

SUNDAY **21**

From *Hazel's Amazing Mother* by Rosemary Wells.

JUNE

June

S	M	T	W	T	F	S
		1	2	3	4	5	6
7	8	9	10	11	12	13
14	15	16	17	18	19	20
21	22	23	24	25	26	27
28	29	30				

MONDAY **22**

TUESDAY **23**

WEDNESDAY **24**

NOTES

_____

_____

_____

_____

THURSDAY **25**

_____

_____

_____

FRIDAY **26**

_____

_____

_____

SATURDAY **27**

_____

_____

SUNDAY **28**

Artwork by Lois Ehlert.

June

S	M	T	W	T	F	S
	1	2	3	4	5	6
7	8	9	10	11	12	13
14	15	16	17	18	19	20
21	22	23	24	25	26	27
28	29	30				

July

S	M	T	W	T	F	S
			1	2	3	4
5	6	7	8	9	10	11
12	13	14	15	16	17	18
19	20	21	22	23	24	25
26	27	28	29	30	31	

August

S	M	T	W	T	F	S
						1
2	3	4	5	6	7	8
9	10	11	12	13	14	15
16	17	18	19	20	21	22
23	24	25	26	27	28	29
30	31					

LOIS EHLERT

"I grew up in a home where everyone seemed to be making something. As long as I can remember, I was always putting things together, cutting, stitching, pasting, or pounding. The 'feel' of the objects I made was as important as the 'look.' "

MONDAY **29**

TUESDAY **30**

WEDNESDAY **1**

THURSDAY **2**

FRIDAY **3**

Independence Day

SATURDAY **4**

SUNDAY **5**

Artwork by Lois Ehlert.

JULY

July

S	M	T	W	T	F	S
			1	2	3	4
5	6	7	8	9	10	11
12	13	14	15	16	17	18
19	20	21	22	23	24	25
26	27	28	29	30	31	

ABOUT LOIS EHLERT

Lois Ehlert was born on November 9, 1934 in Beaver Dam, Wisconsin. The art technique she uses is collage and her distinctive books include *Planting a Rainbow, Color Zoo* and *Feathers for Lunch.*

Although Lois Ehlert did a lot of painting and drawing as she was growing up, she liked cutting and pasting more. If she drew a face, she would never know whether the mouth would look better one inch closer to the nose unless she did the drawing over and over again. But if she made cutouts, she could place them wherever she thought they looked best. She thinks of her vibrantly lush picture books as "little love notes" to children.

MONDAY **6**

TUESDAY **7**

WEDNESDAY **8**

THURSDAY **9**

FRIDAY **10**

SATURDAY **11**

SUNDAY **12**

Artwork by Lois Ehlert.

JULY

July

S	M	T	W	T	F	S
			1	2	3	4
5	6	7	8	9	10	11
12	13	14	15	16	17	18
19	20	21	22	23	24	25
26	27	28	29	30	31	

LOIS EHLERT

"In most cases, my writing goes hand in hand with my art. I work on the writing for a while and then go back to the art. Back and forth, until I get just the right balance. It seems to take me a long time to make a book, and it is difficult but enjoyable work. It's part of a person's make-up, I think, to be creative. It's something I feel very lucky about. I've worked hard to make this gift as fine as I can make it, but I still think I was born with certain ideas and feelings just waiting to burst out!"

MONDAY **13**

TUESDAY **14**

WEDNESDAY **15**

THURSDAY **16**

FRIDAY **17**

SATURDAY **18**

SUNDAY **19**

Artwork by Lois Ehlert.

JULY

July

S	M	T	W	T	F	S
			1	2	3	4
5	6	7	8	9	10	11
12	13	14	15	16	17	18
19	20	21	22	23	24	25
26	27	28	29	30	31	

NOTES

_____

_____

_____

_____

_____

_____

_____

_____

_____

_____

_____

"In time, things will flower,
each in its own way."
—Lois Ehlert

MONDAY **20**

TUESDAY **21**

WEDNESDAY **22**

THURSDAY **23**

FRIDAY **24**

SATURDAY **25**

SUNDAY **26**

How I spent my summer

I got new sneakers

Two teeth fell out

I read books

I ate watermelon

I sweated a lot

I sucked on ice a lot

I wrote three letters — one to my friend, one to an author and one I didn't mail.

I observed nature like my teacher said to do

I went to a birthday party. I ate M&M's and pizza.

I sat in the back of the car a lot

I walked my dog

I looked for toads

I got kissed by visiting relatives a lot

I got two mosquito bites, scabs on my knees and sand in my hair

I met my teacher at the supermarket. I was so surprised!

Some days I missed school

Artwork by Bernard Wa

JULY – AUGUST

July

S	M	T	W	T	F	S
			1	2	3	4
5	6	7	8	9	10	11
12	13	14	15	16	17	18
19	20	21	22	23	24	25
26	27	28	29	30	31	

August

S	M	T	W	T	F	S
						1
2	3	4	5	6	7	8
9	10	11	12	13	14	15
16	17	18	19	20	21	22
23	24	25	26	27	28	29
30	31					

September

S	M	T	W	T	F	S
		1	2	3	4	5
6	7	8	9	10	11	12
13	14	15	16	17	18	19
20	21	22	23	24	25	26
27	28	29	30			

MONDAY **27**

TUESDAY **28**

WEDNESDAY **29**

THURSDAY **30**

FRIDAY **31**

SATURDAY **1**

SUNDAY **2**

BERNARD WABER

"A favorite teacher prescribed reading, observing nature, and writing at least three letters as splendid ways to spend summer—good advice I still follow."

August

S	M	T	W	T	F	S
						1
2	3	4	5	6	7	8
9	10	11	12	13	14	15
16	17	18	19	20	21	22
23	24	25	26	27	28	29
30	31					

ABOUT BERNARD WABER

Bernard Waber was born on September 27, 1924. He was the youngest of four children and grew up in a family that loved to read and draw. His books include the well-known Lyle the crocodile stories, among them *The House on East Eighty-Eighth Street* and *Lyle, Lyle Crocodile*. His house is a "richly endowed museum of crocodilia," including a claw-footed bathtub like the one in the Primm house.

Bernard Waber, who is married and has three children, visits many schools and is always impressed to see children learning, especially reading and writing.

MONDAY **3**

TUESDAY **4**

WEDNESDAY **5**

THURSDAY **6**

FRIDAY **7**

SATURDAY **8**

SUNDAY **9**

From *Lyle Finds His Mother* by Bernard Waber.

AUGUST

August

S	M	T	W	T	F	S
						1
2	3	4	5	6	7	8
9	10	11	12	13	14	15
16	17	18	19	20	21	22
23	24	25	26	27	28	29
30	31					

MONDAY **10**

TUESDAY **11**

WEDNESDAY **12**

THURSDAY **13**

NOTES

_____

_____

_____

_____

_____

_____

_____

_____

_____

FRIDAY **14**

SATURDAY **15**

"There is a freedom about writing that appeals to me. You can do it anywhere— and I have."
—BERNARD WABER

SUNDAY **16**

From *Lyle, Lyle, Crocodile* by Bernard Waber.

AUGUST

August

S	M	T	W	T	F	S
						1
2	3	4	5	6	7	8
9	10	11	12	13	14	15
16	17	18	19	20	21	22
23	24	25	26	27	28	29
30	31					

NOTES

MONDAY **17**

TUESDAY **18**

WEDNESDAY **19**

THURSDAY **20**

FRIDAY **21**

SATURDAY **22**

SUNDAY **23**

From *Lyle Finds His Mother* by Bernard Waber.

AUGUST

August

S	M	T	W	T	F	S
						1
2	3	4	5	6	7	8
9	10	11	12	13	14	15
16	17	18	19	20	21	22
23	24	25	26	27	28	29
30	31					

MONDAY **24**

TUESDAY **25**

WEDNESDAY **26**

THURSDAY **27**

NOTES

_____

_____

_____

_____

_____

_____

_____

_____

_____

_____

_____

FRIDAY **28**

SATURDAY **29**

SUNDAY **30**

Artwork by Tomie dePaola.

August

S	M	T	W	T	F	S
						1
2	3	4	5	6	7	8
9	10	11	12	13	14	15
16	17	18	19	20	21	22
23	24	25	26	27	28	29
30	31					

September

S	M	T	W	T	F	S
		1	2	3	4	5
6	7	8	9	10	11	12
13	14	15	16	17	18	19
20	21	22	23	24	25	26
27	28	29	30			

October

S	M	T	W	T	F	S
				1	2	3
4	5	6	7	8	9	10
11	12	13	14	15	16	17
18	19	20	21	22	23	24
25	26	27	28	29	30	31

TOMIE DePAOLA

"September! How happy I was to have September come. By the middle of August, I was bored and couldn't wait for school to start. If I was lucky enough to get a 'good' teacher, I'd bring her an apple! And then, usually a week or so after school began, it was my BIRTHDAY! Hurray for September!"

MONDAY **31**

TUESDAY **1**

WEDNESDAY **2**

THURSDAY **3**

FRIDAY **4**

SATURDAY **5**

SUNDAY **6**

From *Mary Had a Little Lamb* by Sarah
Josepha Hale, illustrated by Tomie dePaola.

SEPTEMBER

September

S	M	T	W	T	F	S
		1	2	3	4	5
6	7	8	9	10	11	12
13	14	15	16	17	18	19
20	21	22	23	24	25	26
27	28	29	30			

Labor Day

MONDAY **7**

TUESDAY **8**

WEDNESDAY **9**

THURSDAY **10**

FRIDAY **11**

SATURDAY **12**

SUNDAY **13**

ABOUT TOMIE dePAOLA

Born September 15, 1934 in Meriden, Connecticut. Tomie dePaola has over 175 books to his credit.

Tomie dePaola says he remembers the names of all his teachers, he always won spelling bees and his worst subject was arithmetic. He believes a good teacher helps you see yourself. As an artist, he hopes that one of his pictures will touch and change the life of a child for the better.

From *Mary Had a Little Lamb* by Sarah Josepha Hale,
illustrated by Tomie dePaola.

SEPTEMBER

September

S	M	T	W	T	F	S
		1	2	3	4	5
6	7	8	9	10	11	12
13	14	15	16	17	18	19
20	21	22	23	24	25	26
27	28	29	30			

MONDAY **14**

TUESDAY **15**

WEDNESDAY **16**

THURSDAY **17**

NOTES

FRIDAY **18**

SATURDAY **19**

SUNDAY **20**

From *Hey Diddle Diddle & Other Mother Goose Rhymes*,
illustrated by Tomie dePaola.

SEPTEMBER

September

S	M	T	W	T	F	S
		1	2	3	4	5
6	7	8	9	10	11	12
13	14	15	16	17	18	19
20	21	22	23	24	25	26
27	28	29	30			

MONDAY **21**

TUESDAY **22**

WEDNESDAY **23**

THURSDAY **24**

FRIDAY **25**

SATURDAY **26**

SUNDAY **27**

NOTES

Artwork by Steven Kellogg

SEPTEMBER — OCTOBER

September

S	M	T	W	T	F	S
		1	2	3	4	5
6	7	8	9	10	11	12
13	14	15	16	17	18	19
20	21	22	23	24	25	26
27	28	29	30			

October

S	M	T	W	T	F	S
				1	2	3
4	5	6	7	8	9	10
11	12	13	14	15	16	17
18	19	20	21	22	23	24
25	26	27	28	29	30	31

November

S	M	T	W	T	F	S
1	2	3	4	5	6	7
8	9	10	11	12	13	14
15	16	17	18	19	20	21
22	23	24	25	26	27	28
29	30					

STEVEN KELLOGG

"Teachers are, in my opinion, the unsung heroes of our society. They have a profound influence on how we view the world and ourselves in relation to it. They lead us on journeys into the wonders of literature, history, art, and nature, and at the same time they encourage us to explore our inner selves and to discover and to celebrate the qualities that make us special and unique. In my illustration, I focus on the gift that teachers give us when they illuminate the miraculous connections within nature. These sensitive, dedicated, and generous friends deserve our deepest gratitude."

First day of Rosh Hashanah

MONDAY **28**

TUESDAY **29**

WEDNESDAY **30**

THURSDAY **1**

FRIDAY **2**

SATURDAY **3**

SUNDAY **4**

From *Englebert the Elephant* by Tom Paxton,
illustrated by Steven Kellogg.

OCTOBER

October

S	M	T	W	T	F	S
				1	2	3
4	5	6	7	8	9	10
11	12	13	14	15	16	17
18	19	20	21	22	23	24
25	26	27	28	29	30	31

ABOUT STEVEN KELLOGG

Steven Kellogg was born in Norwalk, Connecticut on October 26, 1941. He is married and the father of six stepchildren. Among his popular picture books are stories about the Great Dane Pinkerton, along with *Chicken Little* and *Jimmy's Boa and the Big Splash Birthday Bash*, which he illustrated.

Steven Kellogg has always loved nature and animals and as a child wallpapered his room with animal pictures. He works on his craft every day and says it's easy to work when you enjoy what you do. Steven Kellogg says that he puts love, care, thought and enthusiasm into his work and hopes his readers have a jolly, wonderful and warm reading experience as a result.

MONDAY **5**

TUESDAY **6**

Yom Kippur

WEDNESDAY **7**

THURSDAY **8**

FRIDAY **9**

SATURDAY **10**

SUNDAY **11**

From *Best Friends* by Steven Kellogg.

OCTOBER

October

S	M	T	W	T	F	S
				1	2	3
4	5	6	7	8	9	10
11	12	13	14	15	16	17
18	19	20	21	22	23	24
25	26	27	28	29	30	31

Columbus Day

MONDAY **12**

TUESDAY **13**

WEDNESDAY **14**

THURSDAY **15**

FRIDAY **16**

SATURDAY **17**

SUNDAY **18**

NOTES

From *Best Friends* by Steven Kellogg.

OCTOBER

October

S	M	T	W	T	F	S
				1	2	3
4	5	6	7	8	9	10
11	12	13	14	15	16	17
18	19	20	21	22	23	24
25	26	27	28	29	30	31

NOTES

_____

_____

_____

_____

_____

_____

_____

_____

_____

_____

_____

MONDAY **19**

TUESDAY **20**

WEDNESDAY **21**

THURSDAY **22**

FRIDAY **23**

SATURDAY **24**

SUNDAY **25**

If I Could Create the Perfect Teacher

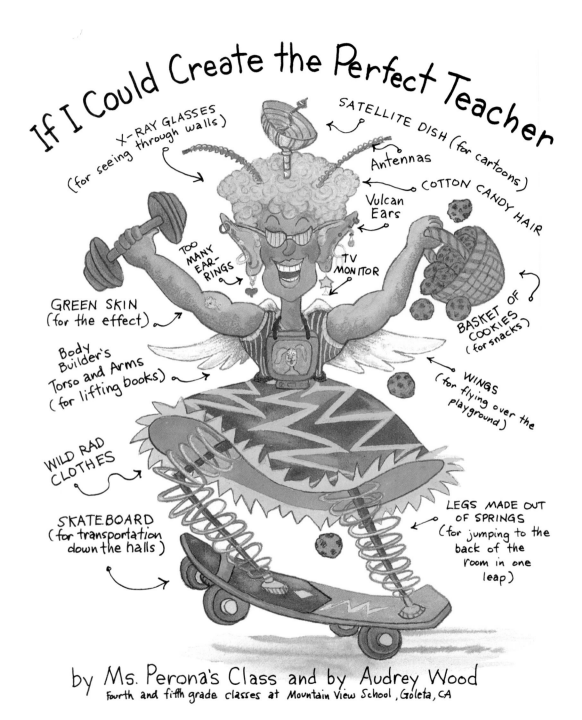

X-RAY GLASSES (for seeing through walls)

SATELLITE DISH (for cartoons)

Antennas

COTTON CANDY HAIR

Vulcan Ears

TOO MANY EAR-RINGS

TV MONITOR

GREEN SKIN (for the effect)

BASKET OF COOKIES (for snacks)

Body Builder's Torso and Arms (for lifting books)

WINGS (for flying over the playground)

WILD RAD CLOTHES

LEGS MADE OUT OF SPRINGS (for jumping to the back of the room in one leap)

SKATEBOARD (for transportation down the halls)

by Ms. Perona's Class and by Audrey Wood
Fourth and fifth grade classes at Mountain View School, Goleta, CA

October

S	M	T	W	T	F	S
				1	2	3
4	5	6	7	8	9	10
11	12	13	14	15	16	17
18	19	20	21	22	23	24
25	26	27	28	29	30	31

November

S	M	T	W	T	F	S
1	2	3	4	5	6	7
8	9	10	11	12	13	14
15	16	17	18	19	20	21
22	23	24	25	26	27	28
29	30					

December

S	M	T	W	T	F	S
		1	2	3	4	5
6	7	8	9	10	11	12
13	14	15	16	17	18	19
20	21	22	23	24	25	26
27	28	29	30	31		

AUDREY WOOD

"My favorite teacher in the second grade served candy corn and bubble gum whistles in little paper cups as a special treat on Fridays.

"My favorite teacher in the fourth grade read novels out loud every day for one hour."

MONDAY **26**

TUESDAY **27**

WEDNESDAY **28**

THURSDAY **29**

FRIDAY **30**

Halloween

SATURDAY **31**

SUNDAY **1**

NOVEMBER

November

S	M	T	W	T	F	S
1	2	3	4	5	6	7
8	9	10	11	12	13	14
15	16	17	18	19	20	21
22	23	24	25	26	27	28
29	30					

ABOUT AUDREY WOOD

Audrey Wood, born in Little Rock, Arkansas on August 12, 1948, lives with her husband and frequent collaborator Don Wood in Santa Barbara, California. She has written and illustrated her own books, including *Weird Parents*, and has written the stories for *The Napping House*, *King Bidgood's in the Bathtub*, a Caldecott Honor Book, and *Heckedy Peg*, all of which Don illustrated. They have over 25 books between them.

Ideas for the Woods' stories come from their idea box, which contains thousands of entries. Audrey Wood hopes that with their books, the real world fades away and their elaborate scenes take over.

MONDAY **2**

Election Day

TUESDAY **3**

WEDNESDAY **4**

THURSDAY **5**

FRIDAY **6**

SATURDAY **7**

SUNDAY **8**

From *Weird Parents* by Audrey Wood.

NOVEMBER

November

S	M	T	W	T	F	S
1	2	3	4	5	6	7
8	9	10	11	12	13	14
15	16	17	18	19	20	21
22	23	24	25	26	27	28
29	30					

MONDAY **9**

TUESDAY **10**

Veterans Day

WEDNESDAY **11**

THURSDAY **12**

NOTES

FRIDAY **13**

SATURDAY **14**

SUNDAY **15**

From *Weird Parents* by Audrey Wood.

NOVEMBER

November

S	M	T	W	T	F	S
1	2	3	4	5	6	7
8	9	10	11	12	13	14
15	16	17	18	19	20	21
22	23	24	25	26	27	28
29	30					

NOTES

_____

_____

_____

_____

_____

_____

_____

_____

_____

_____

MONDAY **16**

TUESDAY **17**

WEDNESDAY **18**

THURSDAY **19**

FRIDAY **20**

SATURDAY **21**

SUNDAY **22**

From *Weird Parents* by Audrey Wood.

NOVEMBER

November

S	M	T	W	T	F	S
1	2	3	4	5	6	7
8	9	10	11	12	13	14
15	16	17	18	19	20	21
22	23	24	25	26	27	28
29	30					

MONDAY **23**

TUESDAY **24**

WEDNESDAY **25**

Thanksgiving

THURSDAY **26**

NOTES

FRIDAY **27**

SATURDAY **28**

SUNDAY **29**

Artwork by Ted Rand.

NOVEMBER — DECEMBER

November

S	M	T	W	T	F	S
1	2	3	4	5	6	7
8	9	10	11	12	13	14
15	16	17	18	19	20	21
22	23	24	25	26	27	28
29	30					

December

S	M	T	W	T	F	S
		1	2	3	4	5
6	7	8	9	10	11	12
13	14	15	16	17	18	19
20	21	22	23	24	25	26
27	28	29	30	31		

January

S	M	T	W	T	F	S
					1	2
3	4	5	6	7	8	9
10	11	12	13	14	15	16
17	18	19	20	21	22	23
24	25	26	27	28	29	30
31						

TED RAND

"Anyone who has ever watched a creature parent teaching its young has clearly seen how much of learning is by example. Remember the line from *My Fair Lady*: 'Don't tell me, show me.' As a teacher I found that showing is believing and sets the stage for learning."

MONDAY **30**

TUESDAY **1**

WEDNESDAY **2**

THURSDAY **3**

FRIDAY **4**

SATURDAY **5**

SUNDAY **6**

DECEMBER

ABOUT TED RAND

Ted Rand, who was born on December 27, 1915, has been married to his wife, Gloria, for 43 years and has two children and one grandchild. Among the books he has illustrated are *Knots on a Counting Rope* and *Barn Dance!* by Bill Martin Jr. and John Archambault.

Although he has had other careers in art, Ted Rand now works exclusively as an illustrator of children's books—and has never enjoyed anything as much. He tries, he says, to enrich his books beyond picturing a story and hopes that his work will trigger more ways of communicating and pursuing relationships. He lives on Mercer Island in Washington, where he was born. He is now collaborating on picture books with his wife, which he says has been a particular pleasure.

MONDAY **7**

TUESDAY **8**

WEDNESDAY **9**

THURSDAY **10**

FRIDAY **11**

SATURDAY **12**

SUNDAY **13**

From *Knots on a Counting Rope* by Bill Martin Jr.
and John Archambault, illustrated by Ted Rand.

DECEMBER

December

S	M	T	W	T	F	S
		1	2	3	4	5
6	7	8	9	10	11	12
13	14	15	16	17	18	19
20	21	22	23	24	25	26
27	28	29	30	31		

NOTES

_____

_____

_____

_____

_____

_____

_____

_____

_____

_____

_____

M O N D A Y **14**

T U E S D A Y **15**

W E D N E S D A Y **16**

T H U R S D A Y **17**

F R I D A Y **18**

S A T U R D A Y **19**

First day of Hanukkah

S U N D A Y **20**

From *Barn Dance!* by Bill Martin Jr. and
John Archambault, illustrated by Ted Rand.

DECEMBER

December

S	M	T	W	T	F	S
		1	2	3	4	5
6	7	8	9	10	11	12
13	14	15	16	17	18	19
20	21	22	23	24	25	26
27	28	29	30	31		

MONDAY **21**

TUESDAY **22**

WEDNESDAY **23**

THURSDAY **24**

Christmas Day

FRIDAY **25**

SATURDAY **26**

SUNDAY **27**

NOTES

From *Salty Takes Off* by Gloria Rand,
illustrated by Ted Rand.

DECEMBER – JANUARY

December

S	M	T	W	T	F	S
		1	2	3	4	5
6	7	8	9	10	11	12
13	14	15	16	17	18	19
20	21	22	23	24	25	26
27	28	29	30	31		

January

S	M	T	W	T	F	S
					1	2
3	4	5	6	7	8	9
10	11	12	13	14	15	16
17	18	19	20	21	22	23
24	25	26	27	28	29	30
31						

February

S	M	T	W	T	F	S
	1	2	3	4	5	6
7	8	9	10	11	12	13
14	15	16	17	18	19	20
21	22	23	24	25	26	27
28						

NOTES

MONDAY **28**

TUESDAY **29**

WEDNESDAY **30**

New Year's Eve

THURSDAY **31**

New Year's Day

FRIDAY **1**

SATURDAY **2**

SUNDAY **3**

Grateful acknowledgment is made to the following publishers for permission to reproduce illustrations originally printed in other books:

BOOKPLATE
HarperCollins Publishers for art on the bookplate page. From *How a Book Is Made* by Aliki. Copyright © 1986 by Aliki Brandenberg.

JANUARY
Alfred A. Knopf, Inc., for art on the pages opposite January 6–26.

FEBRUARY
Dial Books for Young Readers, a division of Penguin Books USA, Inc., for art on the pages opposite February 3–23. From *Pretend You're a Cat* by Jean Marzollo, pictures by Jerry Pinkney. Pictures copyright © 1990 by Jerry Pinkney.

MARCH
Little, Brown and Company Publishers for art on the pages opposite March 2–29.

APRIL
Dial Books for Young Readers, a division of Penguin Books USA, Inc., for art on the page opposite April 6–12. From *The Year of the Perfect Christmas Tree* by Gloria Houston, pictures by Barbara Cooney. Pictures copyright © 1988 by Barbara Cooney.
Viking Penguin, a division of Penguin Books USA, Inc., for art on the page opposite April 13–19. From *Island Boy* by Barbara Cooney. Copyright © 1988 by Barbara Cooney Porter.
Viking Penguin, a division of Penguin Books USA, Inc., for art on the page opposite April 20–26. From *Miss Rumphius* by Barbara Cooney. Copyright © 1982 by Barbara Cooney Porter.

MAY
HarperCollins Publishers for art on the page opposite May 4–10. From *How a Book Is Made* by Aliki. Copyright © 1986 by Aliki Brandenberg.
Greenwillow Books, a division of William Morrow & Co., Inc., for art on the pages opposite May 18–31.

JUNE
Dial Books for Young Readers, a division of Penguin Books USA, Inc., for art on the pages opposite June 8–14 and June 22–28. From *Hazel's Amazing Mother*, copyright © 1985 by Rosemary Wells. All rights reserved. Used with permission.
Dial Books for Young Readers, a division of Penguin Books USA, Inc., for art on the page opposite June 15–21. From *Shy Charles*, copyright © 1988 by Rosemary Wells. All rights reserved. Used with permission.

AUGUST
Houghton Mifflin Company for art on the pages opposite August 3–23.

SEPTEMBER
Holiday House for art on the pages opposite September 7–20. From *Mary Had a Little Lamb*, copyright © 1984 by Tomie dePaola.
The Putnam & Grosset Group for art on the page opposite September 21–27. From *Hey Diddle Diddle & Other Mother Goose Rhymes*, illustrations copyright © 1985 and 1988 (paperback) by Tomie dePaola.

OCTOBER
Morrow Junior Books, a division of William Morrow & Company, Inc., for art on the page opposite October 5–11. Copyright © 1990 by Steven Kellogg.
Dial Books for Young Readers, a division of Penguin Books USA, Inc., for art on the pages opposite October 12–25. From *Best Friends*, copyright © 1986 by Steven Kellogg. All rights reserved. Used with permission.

NOVEMBER
Dial Books for Young Readers, a division of Penguin Books USA, Inc., for art on the pages opposite November 9–29. From *Weird Parents* by Audrey Wood. Copyright © 1990 by Audrey Wood.

DECEMBER
Henry Holt and Company, Inc., for art on the page opposite December 14–20. From *Knots on a Counting Rope* by Bill Martin, Jr. and John Archambault, illustrated by Ted Rand. Illustrations © 1987 by Ted Rand.
Henry Holt and Company, Inc., for art on the page opposite December 21–27. From *Barn Dance!* by Bill Martin, Jr. and John Archambault, illustrated by Ted Rand. Illustrations © 1986 by Ted Rand.
Henry Holt and Company, Inc., for art on the page opposite December 28–January 3. From *Salty Takes Off* by Gloria Rand, illustrated by Ted Rand. Illustrations © 1991 by Ted Rand.

All other art is original.